MW01504237

GROWTH MINDSET DAILY

PERSONAL DEVELOPMENT FOR
EACH DAY OF THE YEAR

Also by DARE ODUYE

Abstract Expressionist Interior Spaces

GROWTH MINDSET DAILY

PERSONAL DEVELOPMENT FOR EACH DAY OF THE YEAR

DARE ODUYE

www.dodezigns.com

Author: Dare Oduye
Cover Design: DoDezigns Ltd
Page layout: DoDezigns Ltd

www.dodezigns.com

ISBN-10: 1717045162
ISBN-13: 978-1717045164

ACKNOWLEDGEMENTS

The whole is greater than the sum of its parts.

This work is a synergistic product of many minds. I have reviewed many years of success literature as part of my own personal development. I am grateful for the inspiration and wisdom of many thinkers for the trans-generational sources and roots of this wisdom.

Special thanks and sincere gratitude is due to the most high God for his Grace, my family, friends and mentors who have provided support both directly and indirectly.

JANUARY

JANUARY

1

Be positive and do everything to the best of your ability. How you do anything is how you do everything.

JANUARY

2

You are more than what you have become. What happens to you does not define who you are and have the potential to be.

JANUARY

3

Be encouraged by your potential daily and the gifts that you have been given to create your best life ever.

JANUARY

4

Your life is a physical representation of your thoughts. Operate with a mentality of abundance. If you think of abundance you will have abundance in your life.

JANUARY

5

Know what you want and have
faith that you can have it. Help people
achieve what they want through a
product or service and then you will
be blessed with what you want.

JANUARY

6

Live honestly with a clear

conscience, so you can enjoy your
happiness and success in peace.

JANUARY

7

Age is nothing but a number. You are as old as the number of experiences you have had, learned and gained wisdom from.

JANUARY

8

Use the unique gifts that God has given to you. What you don't use, you loose.

JANUARY

9

Do not entertain loosing.

Remove loss and defeat from your vocabulary, you either win or learn. Move forward through faith and action to embrace victory.

JANUARY

10

Y ou are the average of the 5

people you spend the most time with.
Choose 5 more people you want to be
like and identify how you can add
value to their lives to create a
commensurate friendship with them.

JANUARY

11

Your enthusiasm represents God within you, always let it shine through. It gives you resilience and strength of character in times of trial.

JANUARY

12

Choose to be happy, no matter what life throws at you acknowledging that God is in control and all things are working in your favour, whether you understand it or not.

JANUARY

13

Adopt a positive outlook on life.

Positive people generally get positive results, while negative people tend to continuously attract negative experiences.

JANUARY

14

Carry your cross daily and fight against the blows that life throws which can dampen your enthusiasm, remember that you are a light of hope and are inspiring many around you.

JANUARY

15

Be still, let go and know that God is in control of your life. Let the creator of all things guide and direct your steps.

JANUARY

16

Winners never quit and quitters never win. Be a winner and never quit!

JANUARY

17

Thoughts become things. Think about winning and believe that God is in the process of helping you to win.

JANUARY

18

Efficient people operate with a grace that helps them to do things easily without struggle.

JANUARY
19

Provide support and offer help for others in need. This will give you greater perspective and exposure to deal with your own challenges.

JANUARY

20

Everything you need is already within you. Accumulated knowledge will provide heightened awareness of their presence.

JANUARY

21

Love yourself and acknowledge that God, made no mistake in creating you. You are made whole and perfect in the image of the creator.

JANUARY

22

Knowing that God is on your side produces a self assured aura of confidence in all of your dealings.

JANUARY

23

Faith is like a muscle and grows stronger through regular use and exertion. Like a muscle it deteriorates and wastes away if unused.

JANUARY
24

Your words hold power that can create both life and death. Each morning speak life over every area of your life.

JANUARY

25

Knowing how to handle and overcome challenges brings about confidence and assertiveness.

JANUARY

26

Each day arise and affirm out loud "I am blessed and highly favoured" three times.

JANUARY

27

Your state dictates your feelings; this then creates behaviours that drive results. You can therefore reverse engineer the results you want by identifying the state required to achieve it.

JANUARY

28

It is better to focus on and
celebrate the strengths of people
rather than trying to change them or
spending much time addressing their
weaknesses.

JANUARY
29

Condition your determination and resilience by affirming three times out loud every morning "I can, I will, I must".

JANUARY

30

Enthusiasm is contagious and spreads like an engulfing wildfire adding great warmth, energy and vitality to personal/business relationships and physical well-being.

JANUARY

31

Start with the end in mind, by envisioning the goal you would like to achieve in detail. Start each day by taking a trip into your future. Visualise all sensory elements, smells, sights/colours, feelings, sounds and tastes.

FEBRUARY

FEBRUARY

1

When you realise that you have the Creator on your side, defeat no longer becomes an option.

FEBRUARY

2

Your mind is a navigational device waiting for you to boldly choose a destination. You do not need to know every route or direction. The why and will to want, will create the how. Just decide where you want to go.

FEBRUARY

3

Exercise, rest and diet all
contribute to your physical well-being.
However, your mental and spiritual
states are also key to overall good
health.

FEBRUARY

4

Set ambitious goals through faith in all areas of your life, such as your career, family, studies, finances and health. Affirm grateful acceptance of these goals three times each day.

FEBRUARY

5

People do things based on their current level of understanding. If they knew better, they would do better.

FEBRUARY

6

Blessings and opportunities can sometimes be gift wrapped in problems. There is always a useful lesson for us to take away from them that can help build character.

FEBRUARY

7

Communicate with and then quickly forgive those who may have offended you. Grudges weigh down and dampen your spirit. They sap you of energy that could be used for worthy pursuits.

FEBRUARY

8

Do not allow money to become your master. You're time is valuable and can never be bought. Money is simply a resource that provides options. Instead, be disciplined, refrain from instant gratification, master money and have it work for you.

FEBRUARY

9

Faith without works is dead. A strong faith must be supported by action.

FEBRUARY

10

Start with an inside out paradigm shift. If you want things to change around you, you must change yourself first.

FEBRUARY

11

Work on yourself first and you will then attract things commensurate with your new and heightened level of awareness.

FEBRUARY

12

Y ou we're born with potential power to handle all situations and circumstances. This power is made stronger through use. Believe that God will never put you in a situation that you cannot handle.

FEBRUARY

13

Spend some time with yourself. It is easy to become distracted and so busy that we forget to turn off all devices, be still, meditate or pray and listen. Pick a set time in your day, preferably first thing in the morning to do this.

FEBRUARY

14

Affirm each day that you deserve to live a life full of joy, love, happiness and success.

FEBRUARY

15

Be solution orientated. When problems arise, do not procrastinate with a victim mentality, move with swift action and focus on solving them.

FEBRUARY

16

The physical transformation first takes place in the renewed mind. Visualise your desired form daily to keep motivated.

FEBRUARY

17

Rediscover purpose and regularly get involved in philanthropic causes much bigger than yourself. It is your social responsibility to give back. Doing this will also reignite your energy levels.

FEBRUARY

18

Be positive, optimistic and
expect the best that life has to offer.

FEBRUARY

19

To get the best out of people become a merchant of hope. People are motivated by a strong why. Help them to realise the root cause and driver for their actions.

FEBRUARY

20

Your life is a physical representation of your thoughts. Everything you think about is attracted to you.

FEBRUARY

21

Rest assured that all of your needs will be met and taken care of by God.

FEBRUARY

22

Even when people upset or offend you, continue to show them love. Pray for them, with an understanding that you also make mistakes.

FEBRUARY

23

Your mind is like a garden. A mental garden. The books we read, the things we watch and listen too plant seeds that take root and bear fruit in our lives. Be intentional about what you want to manifest in your life. Be deliberate about what you expose yourself too.

FEBRUARY

24

Believe in yourself and become your biggest fan. You may not be where you want to be but remind yourself that you are masterpiece in progress.

FEBRUARY

25

People can only offend you with your permission. Insults can only be given power if you accept them. If you do not respond to or acknowledge them they remain powerless and void.

FEBRUARY

26

Have an unshakeable belief in God.

FEBRUARY

27

S uccess is different for everyone.

It lies in steady progression towards a personal goal. Therefore, to remain successful continue to set new goals after every achievement.

FEBRUARY

28

Write down your vision and make it clear. This is of upmost importance when leading a team. Communicate the vision regularly, this helps provide hope.

FEBRUARY

29

Fear is the corruption of faith. Do not be imprisoned by fear, it binds people to lower levels of existence by the shackles of their mind.

MARCH

MARCH

1

Just as you put rubbish in the bin and throw it away once full, frequently detox your mind from anything that is contrary to the greater vision you have for yourself.

MARCH

2

Do your best in everything that you do, take pride in the signature trademark you create whenever you carry out a task or people deal with you. Be known for excellence.

MARCH

3

Be positive in all things, expecting positive results in everything you do.

MARCH

4

Put things into perspective.

When met with challenging situations, release yourself from a negative response by considering how important or insignificant the outcome of the situation will be in a years time.

MARCH

5

Be B.O.L.D in all things. Bravely, Overcome, Limiting, Distractions.

MARCH

6

God the creator and father, has made all things. If you need anything, don't be afraid to ask him and expect receipt as a rightful heir.

MARCH

7

Face your fears and tackle your obstacles head on. Overcoming these vices will liberate and empower you. You will then realise how theses vices have been stopping you from living your best life.

MARCH

We seek guidance from a manufacturer when we want to learn more about a product. How much more should we seek the creator when we want to learn more about how we can get the best out of our lives.

MARCH

9

Everything that comes out of your mouth you give life to so, focus your energy on what you want. Avoid talking, thinking or worrying about the things you don't want.

MARCH

10

Wake up every day and
practice good habits. The first hour of
your day is golden and helps shape
the direction of your day and
life. Avoid negative media; fill yourself
with good, positive and wholesome
input.

MARCH

11

Anger puts out the lamp in your mind, prevents rational thought patterns and subsequently affects your judgement. Avoid making important decisions when overcome by this emotion. Rather channel this energy into a positive physical motion such as exercise.

MARCH

12

Emotions are simply energy in motion, this energy should always be transformed and used for your benefit.

MARCH

13

All things are possible to you, if you just believe. The word impossible, plainly reads "I'm-possible".

MARCH

14

We navigate towards and become the vision we see for ourselves. Create a vision board of your desired image. Be bold and daring in the production of this vision and don't worry if you're not where you want to be. Take a trip into your future by looking at the desired vision each day.

MARCH

15

Affirm that you are an heir to everything that is good, lovely and desirable. Affirm that you are happy and grateful to be in receipt of these things through faith.

MARCH

16

Frame problems and challenges as tools to sharpen your faith, intelligence and creativity. Recognise that there are always solutions and they are waiting for you to find them.

MARCH

17

Become comfortable being uncomfortable. Growth and development come through struggle. Before any living thing bears fruit or transforms to an elevated state, it experiences discomfort at its highest tolerance level. Casing points are labour and the metamorphosis of a caterpillar to a butterfly.

MARCH

18

Embrace turbulence. As a plane travels with speed, and is just about to take flight, everything in the environment shakes. In life this turbulence occurs when, the things that are limiting you are about to be overcome by your higher elevated state.

MARCH

19

You can't see the picture when you're in the frame. Be sure to regularly take a step back review things from a different perspective.

MARCH

20

Cherish positive experiences in an archive of joy producing experiences, that you can reflect on for reinvigoration when needed.

MARCH

21

If you just believe that you can overcome any setback, your creative potential will then help you.

MARCH

22

Act and carry yourself in accordance with the higher vision you hold for yourself.

MARCH

23

If you try to chase two things at the same time, both will evade you.

MARCH

24

Once you've set yourself a goal, F.O.C.U.S on it. You must Follow One Course Until Successful.

MARCH

25

Worrying does not solve problems; neither does it add joy, peace or happiness to you. It will not help you experience life at a greater level. It is a form of procrastination that stops you from taking control of your life.

Y ou have a choice in everything.

Never operate with a victims mentality. Take control and full responsibility for everything that happens to/for you.

MARCH

27

Take nothing for granted and hold nothing back. Give your all, as if each day was your last.

MARCH

28

Be grateful for everything.

MARCH

29

Cast away any antagonistic thoughts of defeat or lack from your mind.

MARCH

30

Transform yourself through a renewed positive, abundance framed mindset. You will then attract commensurate people and circumstances in line with this. You will also witness that things no longer in sync with your new way of thinking, eventually drift away.

MARCH

31

Encourage yourself by acknowledging your current blessings, opportunities and possibilities.

APRIL

APRIL

1

The amount of joy, love, peace and happiness you create in the lives of other people is directly proportional to the amount you will have in your own life.

APRIL

2

Take care of yourself, so that you can take even better care of others.

APRIL

3

All of your electrical devices need charging to remain functional. Recharge yourself every morning and evening through prayer. This will empower you to operate at peak performance and provide numerous health benefits.

APRIL

4

Whenever, you have to carry out a task that you do not enjoy, reframe the activity by remembering that you get to do it. There is someone who would love to do what you call drudgery.

APRIL

5

Peace is a fruit of the presence of God. Peace creates the perfect environment for self-healing which can resolve a number of illnesses.

APRIL

6

To improve your creative capacity, remove all traces of fear. Creativity is developed in an environment of faith and positivity.

APRIL

7

Fear can bring to pass things that are feared. Do not fear.

APRIL

8

Like God the creator, we are also creators, have been designed to take conscious charge of our thoughts and direct them to our desired goals.

APRIL

9

It is your rightful duty to be happy and successful.

APRIL

10

Your energy and presence are your signature. People remember how you make them feel. So, make sure your imprint and memory sheds warmth over everyone you meet.

APRIL
11

Remind yourself everyday that God wants you to have the best and you deserve to receive the best.

APRIL

12

What you know has got you to where you are. To have more you have to know more and operate differently to the way you are now.

APRIL

13

The challenges you currently face have been created by the level of knowledge you presently have. To solve them you have to gain additional knowledge.

APRIL

14

Make sure your goals are clear, sharp, definite and specific. Combine prayer, diligent smart application of your efforts along regular visualisation of the end goal for encouragement.

APRIL

15

The one consistent trait in every successful person is the ability to persevere.

APRIL

16

Make hope a daily habit. It will help uplift your spirit.

APRIL

17

Use the unlimited power of faith to keep you resilient. With faith nothing can keep you down.

APRIL

18

Make sure that you clear your mind from all worries before going to sleep each night. Love yourself enough to resolve any disagreements you may have had, so that you can keep your peace, are not weighed down by the burden of strife and wake up restored and well rested.

APRIL

19

Do not worry about tomorrow.

Affirm that God has equipped you to handle anything that may come your way.

APRIL

20

Enthusiastic ideas dominate thoughts and create the ideal environment for innovation and new opportunities.

APRIL

21

God's blessings do not only relate to financial gain. God's blessings will make you prosperous in all areas of life.

APRIL

22

The first secret to success is self belief. You can achieve amazing things with self belief.

APRIL

23

Sometimes you have to slow down to speed up.

APRIL

24

Enthusiasm is magical. Its contagious power influences and drives people to action.

APRIL

25

Take life on with the energy and determination of a roaring lion when pursuing its prey. You've got to be hungry. Make your goal, your prey and take it by force.

APRIL

26

Take steps to live a sustainable lifestyle, improve your health, vitality and overall wellbeing today.

APRIL
27

Success is the progressive
realisation of a worthy ideal.

APRIL

28

When you are engaged in something you believe in, you will have increased vigour and energy. You will notice that you passionately throw yourself into it for extended periods without feeling tired.

APRIL

29

Your mental image is made up by your thoughts and words. You become like your mental image, so always think and speak positivity. April 30 - Make a commitment to ensure every word that comes out of your mouth edifies others and plants positive seeds that will reap good fruit for all who hear.

MAY

MAY

1

Possibilities lie in all things that challenge us. When you believe without doubt, the possibilities will present themselves.

MAY

2

Our greatest strength as human beings lies within our faith. It is a powerful force that can move mountains.

MAY

3

Anything in your life that has been a stumbling block has been empowered by your choice to become a victim to it. Positively declare your freedom and your consciousness will respond accordingly.

MAY

Find your personal "why" and let it fuel your ambition.

MAY

5

Life is like a personal trainer who occasionally throws difficulties at us to strengthen and stretch our mental muscles.

Remove lack, loss and limitations from your mental image.

MAY

7

Motivation is like prescribed medication. It must be administered and taken daily.

MAY

8

The presence of God is denoted by an overwhelming peace that cannot be understood. It is a quiet power that relieves all tension and stress.

MAY

9

our thoughts can either make you sick or well. Choose healthy thoughts.

MAY

10

Take 5 minutes out of your day each morning, free from distractions to just clear your mind and be still.

MAY

11

It's best to surround yourself with those who have the same vision as you, rather than trying to impose your ideas on naysayers. Let them come around in their own time. Remember that those persuaded against their will are of the same opinion still.

MAY

12

When working towards your higher vision, expect opposition but remember that eagles and pigeons have two different visions. Eagles are uncommon and possess great vision. Be like the eagle.

MAY

13

Don't let fear cause you to miss out on the grand blessings available to you. God can bless you commensurate with the level of your belief.

MAY

14

Prayer is the act of opening your mind to hear the voice of God. God can talk to you in different ways and at different times. Identify your best way to hear from God.

MAY

15

Operate with a spirit of gratitude and expectancy in all things.

MAY

16

How the world responds to us is based on our outlook and attitude to the world. There is no fire without fuel. To get the best from life, we first have to give and expect the best.

MAY

17

Treat everyone meet with respect and honour. Treat them like the most important person in the world. They are.

MAY

18

The greatest need of all people is to feel appreciated.

MAY

19

If you want to improve and change any area of your life, you need to start with making changes in yourself. Become the change you want to be via an inside out paradigm shift.

MAY

20

Success is not defined by the achievement of a goal. Success is defined by the journey and process of working towards a goal. Therefore, to remain successful continue to set yourself new goals that you will work towards.

MAY

21

Never procrastinate; there is never a right time to do the right thing. Tomorrow never comes. Do it now.

MAY

22

When blessed with an idea, take action and just do it. Over thinking and excessive analysis can cause you to doubt yourself. Doubt takes you out of action and action takes you out of doubt.

MAY

23

How you do anything, is how you will do everything. Give your best in everything that you do.

MAY

24

Invest in yourself. Challenge yourself to learn something new everyday. Adopt a passion for continuous daily development and learning.

MAY

25

What you read pours massive ingredients into your mind and your life will be built from those ingredients.

MAY

26

It's the little foxes that spoil the vines. Be aware of your bad habits and limiting beliefs. If not overcome and left unchecked QA habits can hamper your productivity.

MAY

27

There are no elevators to your goal. You have to take the stairs. You need to need to take thoughtful action to achieve your goals. It may not be easy but it will be worth it.

MAY

28

To reignite your enthusiasm, spend more time in prayer and meditation.

MAY

29

Whether you think you can, or whether you think you can't, you are right. Take control of your thoughts and adopt a positive can-do attitude no matter what.

MAY

30

When faced with challenges and trials, be-persistent. Never give up, keep going. When facing setbacks learn from these experiences and keep trying. Interpret setbacks as feedback encouraging you to change your approach.

MAY

31

Whenever you pray, be thankful and expect to receive everything you need.

JUNE

JUNE

1

Always think and talk abundance
for in doing so you are decreeing
abundance.

JUNE

2

You have to believe you have already won in your mind way before the event to pick up the prize.

JUNE

3

See your ideal self and practice being it.

JUNE

4

Only think of positive outcomes.

JUNE

5

Contact with God is what gives you the special grace, energy and flow to create and bring forth new things.

JUNE

6

Motivation creates a fire within you. Your why will keep it burning and bring out your inner power.

JUNE

7

Spiritual principles help you tap into the power of your mind. Combined with faith you can manifest extraordinary results.

JUNE

8

Free your mind and conscience from all grudges and non-progressive thoughts. A clean mind is the best environment to tap into your creative powers.

JUNE

9

Pain helps us to grow. It is inevitable and can't be avoided. Every day you have to choose between the pain of discipline and the pain of regret.

JUNE

10

Practice silence daily to develop a peaceful mind. Doing so will help you to appreciate the subtle sounds of harmony and natural beauty around you.

JUNE

11

Be humble, kind and mature in mind and soul. People like and respond better to others with these personality traits.

JUNE

12

You tend to find what you're looking for. There is good in everything and everyone, look for the good in all things.

JUNE

13

Help other people overcome worrying. In helping others overcome worry, you become better at overcoming it yourself.

JUNE

14

The seed of greatness lies within every living thing. Stay away from oxymoronic seedless fruit.

JUNE

15

Change your perception. If you change the way you look at things, then the things you look at will change.

JUNE

16

All things are possible, if you just believe.

JUNE

17

Private victories are achieved by practicing your craft. Consistent private victories will eventually bring about public victory and recognition.

JUNE

18

Take full responsibility for everything you're involved in, whether the outcome is good or bad.

JUNE

19

Find something complimentary to say about every person that you meet.

JUNE

20

Your greatness is on the other side of fear.

JUNE

21

Get comfortable seeking advice from God as you would an advisor or professional. He is the manufacturer of the universe and hears your calling.

JUNE

22

You will find fun and pleasure engaging in your true calling.

JUNE

23

Water your mind with enriching and uplifting material and consciously monitor what you expose yourself to so that the weeds of negative thoughts don't destroy the garden of your life.

JUNE

24

Where will you be 5 years from now if you continue what you're doing now? If you don't like that prospective vision, change what you're doing right now.

JUNE

25

Look for beauty in everything.

Look for the equal opposite benefit in every adversity.

JUNE
26

Y ou are exactly where you have

chosen to be in life. For a better life, simply make better choices.

JUNE

27

You are alive for a purpose.

Remember God doesn't build stairways that lead nowhere.

JUNE

28

Your success is directly proportional to your ability to sell. You are constantly selling yourself, your values, philosophy, vision, goals, time, services or products to the world around you.

JUNE

29

Show love and you will receive love. This will allow you to experience joy and become a cheerful person.

JUNE

30

Everyday remind yourself that you deserve the best and are going to get the best out of life.

JULY

JULY

1

Affirm daily your gratitude for attracting all the good fortune, opportunities and people required to help you live your best life ever.

JULY

2

Be grateful when facing challenge and adversity. Reframe the situation by acknowledging that things will get better.

JULY

3

Spiritual motivation is the most powerful form of motivation.

JULY

4

The world in which you live can be changed by repeatedly painting a clear, emotive vision on the canvas in your mind.

JULY

5

Always remember that every cloud has a silver lining.

JULY

6

Prayer is a two-way conversation between yourself and God. After you have spoken, its best to just be still and listen for answers, guidance and direction.

JULY

7

The presence of God in your mind, body and spirit will give you health and energy.

JULY

8

Happiness is experienced when you forgive quickly, avoid worry, give more than you expect to receive and live simply.

JULY

9

Discard your old mindset and be transformed by the renewing of your mind through a new positive outlook.

JULY

10

To produce effective actions, think positively about your abilities.

JULY

11

Believe in God and in yourself and your life can be everything you want it to be.

JULY

12

When you find an inspiring idea, it will motivate and fill you with dynamic energy.

JULY

13

Visualise want you want in your mind and the visualisation will be actualised.

JULY

14

Who you are right now, has attracted what you have. To have more you have to become more.

JULY

15

Sometimes the best way to solve an ongoing problem is to temporarily focus on something else and then return with a fresh pair of eyes. The break away will give you renewed insight.

JULY

16

Eat healthy, exercise daily, ensure you have adequate rest, think positively, work hard, pray and love often.

JULY

17

Affirm daily that you're going to make it no matter what. It won't always be easy and challenges will arise but remember that you are still going to make it.

JULY

18

Sometimes, God will allow things to appear impossible or insurmountable because he wants you to recognise that your victory can only come from him.

JULY

19

Success is not easy to achieve.

However, ease is a greater hindrance to success than hardship.

JULY

20

You have two eyes, ears and one mouth so that you can watch and listen, twice as much as you talk.

JULY

21

Fill your mind with what you want more of. To have a peaceful existence, fill your mind with peace

JULY

22

Always be true to yourself. Listen to your own instincts; it serves as a guiding beacon towards inner peace.

JULY

23

The most beautiful and cherished elements in this world have the humblest and most challenging journeys. When facing difficulty, remember that diamonds are formed under heat and pressure.

JULY

24

Fruitful productivity and growth can only be gained through resistance and pain. Reframe your perception of pain and discomfort. Embrace it, by acknowledging you are getting better in every way.

JULY

25

Affirm every morning, that you are getting better in every way, day by day.

JULY

26

Upon waking up each morning, celebrate with enthusiasm and excitement for the God given gift and opportunity that is the present.

JULY

27

Be courageous and strong.

Everything you do will be victorious with the help of God.

JULY

28

Affirm daily, that you are blessed and highly favoured.

JULY

29

Be bold and live life to the fullest.

JULY
30

When opportunity presents itself, overcome doubt, fear of risk and give it ago. Life is the riskiest opportunity of them all. You don't get out of life alive.

JULY

31

There are no guarantees in life; everything has an element of risk. Trying to avoid risk can limit you from living life to the fullest.

AUGUST

AUGUST

1

Show people that you believe in them. Become a merchant of hope and make people aware of the infinite potential within them. Doing this will also empower you.

AUGUST

2

Changing your thinking from wrong to right, from error to truth is the secret to successful living.

AUGUST

3

When you are doing your best and expecting positive results, God will meet your needs through your efforts.

AUGUST

4

Always be present. Wherever you are and whatever you are doing, be 100% there. Give your full attention and energy to the present.

AUGUST

5

Learn from your mistakes and try again.

AUGUST

6

Success is going from failure to failure without discouragement.

AUGUST

7

Don't make judgements according to appearances. You have to walk by faith not sight.

AUGUST

Adversity does not come to stay, it comes to pass.

AUGUST

9

Nothing works unless you work. You are the common denominator.

AUGUST

10

Life is not a dress rehearsal; you don't get a chance to do it again. Make the most of every opportunity.

AUGUST

11

There is no such thing as tomorrow. Tomorrow never comes. The best way to avoid doing something is to put it off until "tomorrow". It will not get done because tomorrow never comes, there is only today. Do not procrastinate.

AUGUST

12

Life is about choices. You decide how you choose to respond to events. Choose to be happy.

AUGUST

13

Success is looking for a good place to stay. It is attracted to the type of person you are now becoming.

AUGUST
14

When presented with an opportunity, don't focus too much on what you can't get. Focus more so on what you can offer, what the opportunity will make of you and who you will become in the process.

AUGUST

15

If you worry about past or future events you waste mental energy that would be better used focusing on today for a better tomorrow.

AUGUST

16

God rewards those who love and diligently seek him.

AUGUST

17

There is nothing more expensive than a missed opportunity because of a closed mind. Always be open minded to new opportunities and try to see things from a different perspective.

AUGUST

18

You get paid for the value you bring to the market place. To earn more, provide greater value in your service. Help more people achieve what they want and then you will have everything you want.

AUGUST

19

In chaotic moments, be still and let your inner inspiration rise. This will provide an inflow of new clear thoughts.

AUGUST

20

Affirm daily that you will only give energy to thoughts that serve you.

AUGUST

21

When you react you are giving away your power. When you respond you are staying in control of yourself.

AUGUST

22

Always remember that believing
is seeing. You have to see yourself
living out your vision in your minds
eye before you can see it in reality.

AUGUST

23

Always do things with high
energy, passion and enthusiasm. If
you're casual about life, you will
become a casualty.

AUGUST

24

If used correctly, your voice can impact people. It can change their awareness, influence and persuade them.

AUGUST

25

Good presentations empower
people's psychology and physiology
consequently influencing them to a
specific call of action.

AUGUST

26

The difference between the wealthiest and most successful people in the world, is how they use their 24 hours.

AUGUST

27

Take a look at your daily routine and ask yourself how you can leverage yourself. How can you produce more in less time? What systems can you put in place to efficiently maximise your time?

AUGUST

28

There is never a right time to do the right thing. If you know you should do something, do it now.

AUGUST

29

Create a mastermind of like minded people and those who you can both learn from and add value to. This group should hold you accountable to a higher standard.

AUGUST

30

Examine your expectations versus your wishes. Some people wish to do better and others expect to do better. Always expect to do better.

AUGUST
31

Love yourself enough to take time out for yourself. You can't be a high achiever if you don't feel good. Take care of yourself.

SEPTEMBER

SEPTEMBER

1

Develop compassion for yourself despite your imperfections. Be gentle with yourself, it's okay to make mistakes as long as you learn from them.

SEPTEMBER

2

Be clear and specific about what you want from every interaction. Always be specific and intentional about your life.

SEPTEMBER

3

Wandering generalities are tossed to and throw during winds of change. Set your sail in line with your predefined goals and objectives so that you can use turbulent winds to steer you towards your goals.

SEPTEMBER

4

If you fail, just learn from the experience. Don't worry about it. To "fail" is describes as the "First Attempt In Learning".

SEPTEMBER

5

Learn to identify diamonds in their rough state. Everything you need lies within you. Don't be led astray by what appears to be greener pastures. The grass is green where it is most watered and taken care of.

SEPTEMBER

6

There are no limitations except those you set yourself. Both poverty and riches are the direct results of your thoughts.

SEPTEMBER

7

Be persistent and remember that most people will say no seven times before they say yes. When presenting your business offering, idea, product or opportunity persistently operates with enthusiasm and optimism without discouragement.

SEPTEMBER

9

The peace of God is medicinal. It can be a better healer than medicine for calming nerves and tension.

SEPTEMBER

9

You will never know what great things you can do until you really try.

SEPTEMBER

10

Never take no for an answer. It simply means, next opportunity.

SEPTEMBER

11

What you dwell on is who you become.

SEPTEMBER

12

It's easier to find balance when you focus your eyes on one thing.

SEPTEMBER

13

We act, feel and perform in accordance with what we imagine to be true about ourselves and our environment.

SEPTEMBER

14

Those who do not increase you
will inevitably decrease you.

SEPTEMBER

15

People who respect themselves and their abilities help nurture your capabilities and your self esteem.

SEPTEMBER

16

Celebrate your individuality, acknowledge that you are unique and were intentionally created to be different.

SEPTEMBER

17

Your mind is your strongest asset, nourish it daily.

SEPTEMBER

18

Make today the day you put aside all that worried or upset you yesterday.

SEPTEMBER
19

Overcome any thought, feeling of past hurt or any remembrance or disappointment.

SEPTEMBER

20

Acknowledge that you have within you all the qualities you need to be happy, to be fulfilled and to be successful in all of your undertakings.

SEPTEMBER

21

The only thing keeping you from what you want is the story you keep telling yourself about why you don't have it.

SEPTEMBER

22

The food you eat can either be the safest and most powerful form of medicine or the slowest form of poison.

SEPTEMBER

23

Take the first step in faith, you don't need to see the whole staircase, just take the first step.

SEPTEMBER

24

There are no shortcuts. It takes time to build, a better, stronger version of yourself.

SEPTEMBER

25

You automatically take on the habits and power of the people you associate with. Control this by forming a Master Mind Group, who can assist you to achieve your dreams.

SEPTEMBER

26

Rise up and attack the day with enthusiasm.

SEPTEMBER

27

Today is another chance, make yourself proud and do the right things.

SEPTEMBER

28

In depth spiritual experiences change things for you. They reinvigorate and keep you alive every day.

SEPTEMBER

29

To remain positive, you have to be a tough minded, hard headed realist. You have to see the solutions in difficulties.

SEPTEMBER

30

Problems help keep you alive. If you don't have them, you're not living.

OCTOBER

OCTOBER

1

If you're not continually facing new things, you're not living you're repeating.

OCTOBER

2

Renew your power daily by allocating time to be still, relax and open yourself to the flow of Gods power.

OCTOBER

3

Make self motivation and personal growth apart of your daily routine. Just as you wouldn't go a day without water, don't go a day without exposing yourself to motivation material.

OCTOBER

4

Remove thoughts of lack from your mind and refill with thoughts of abundance.

OCTOBER

5

Expect generous blessings in unending supply.

OCTOBER

6

Challenge yourself to be what your higher self knows you ought to be; challenge yourself to be the best human being you can be.

OCTOBER

7

All the enthusiasm you need lies within you. Unleash it and let the contagious fire of motivation warm all.

OCTOBER

8

Focused and diligent hard work is a mandatory part of achieving your goals but make sure you have fun in the process. You have to enjoy it to endure.

OCTOBER

9

Allow God to operate through your mind by keeping yourself pure, free from anything that may contaminate your mind, body, spirit and soul.

OCTOBER

10

Identify the things in your life that block communion with God and remove them. These things block access to your power.

OCTOBER

11

Look for the best in everything and everyone you meet. Draw the best out through encouragement and edification.

OCTOBER

12

Always put your best foot forward. Approach each day and groom yourself daily as though you were going to meet the most important person in the world.

OCTOBER

13

Remind yourself of your predetermined victory. You can if you believe you can.

OCTOBER

14

Your results are directly proportional to your level of faith.

OCTOBER

15

One rotten apple in a bowl of apples will eventually contaminate and cause the decay of all other apples in close proximity. Bad company will corrupt good character. Be aware of your environment.

OCTOBER

16

Resentment and grudges weigh down the spirit sap you of energy and dampen your enthusiasm. Love yourself enough to avoid those leeches of energy.

OCTOBER

17

Start your day, week, month and year once you have finished designing it. Be proactive and live an intentionally well-designed life by planning everything.

OCTOBER

18

Don't worry about what may not go according to plan, become excited by the various positive outcomes.

OCTOBER

19

Accept that things do not happen to you, they happen for you.

OCTOBER

20

Move with increased confidence knowing that life is on your side and planning everything in your favour.

OCTOBER

21

Affirm daily that you are a winner, a champion, a victor destined to be successful in all things.

OCTOBER

22

There is nothing new under the sun. Don't reinvent the wheel. Every innovation or "new thing" has been inspired or influenced by a precedent. Use the wheel and think about how you can personalise it.

OCTOBER

23

Adversity reveals your true character. It introduces you to who you really are as a person.

OCTOBER
24

Your major groundbreaking idea is in your mind. Begin the excavation of ideas in your mind by thinking daily.

OCTOBER

25

Free up time first thing in the
morning to exercise your mind. Do
this by picking an area of your life and
thinking of 10 ways to improve it, so
that you can develop and experience
life at a higher level.

OCTOBER

26

Visualise yourself filled with energy, vitality and zeal for life.

OCTOBER

27

Be excited about life. Remind yourself of all your happiest moments multiple times each day.

OCTOBER

28

How you respond to a problem is more important than the problem itself.

OCTOBER

29

To have more than you have right now, you have to become more than you are.

OCTOBER

30

People are not interested in what you know or can offer until they know that you care about their own interests first.

OCTOBER
31

People envy those they want to be like. Whether they are willing to admit it or not, people only hate those they want to be like.

NOVEMBER

NOVEMBER

1

Encourage yourself through positive affirmations daily. When experiencing difficulty, boldly speak life giving and empowering words to yourself to victoriously overcome the situation.

NOVEMBER

2

To have peaceful relationships, you have to sacrifice individual selfishness for commensurate gain.

NOVEMBER

3

Set yourself ambitious goals but partition those goals into manageable milestones. Celebrate each milestone on route to achieving the larger goal. This way you motivate yourself to work towards the larger goal through regular reward.

NOVEMBER

4

Humble self confidence is borne when you realise that your victory and success comes from God.

NOVEMBER

5

The spirit of enthusiasm will give you a sparkle in your eye and charismatic charm.

NOVEMBER

6

Like an elastic band you demonstrate your true potential when stretched. You were not created to stay in a comfortable, dormant state.

NOVEMBER

7

Peaceful thoughts and words have strange healing power.

NOVEMBER

8

Navigate life with meaningful specificity, do not be a wandering generality. Be clear about what it is that you want. Be intentional and deliberate about how you live your life.

NOVEMBER

9

There is nothing to lose in following your heart, only much to gain.

NOVEMBER

10

You are either adding value to your environment, friendships, relationships and business or you are diminishing it. Become a person of value.

NOVEMBER
11

The road to greatness is not immediate, common or approved by everyone. It can be a lonely road that requires sustained perseverance.

NOVEMBER

12

If you are not mentally ready, you are never really physically prepared.

NOVEMBER

13

Limiting habits or behaviours in your personality type, that you aren't aware of may hold you back. Regularly touch base with an accountability partner who can help you see these behaviours and consequently boost your personal development.

NOVEMBER

14

To overcome your fears, force yourself to repeatedly do the things you're afraid of.

NOVEMBER
15

When going through difficulty, remember your strong purpose, it will pull you through and help you see the bigger picture.

NOVEMBER

16

Self confidence comes from feeling good about yourself. It is built by the good feelings created by doing what you know you should do and carrying out daily disciplines.

NOVEMBER
17

Self confidence comes from the willingness and can-do attitude to overcome challenges.

NOVEMBER

18

Enthusiasm stems from self confidence.

NOVEMBER

19

Enthusiasm will motivate you to be the best you possibly can.

NOVEMBER

20

Life does not waste success on the unprepared. Prepare yourself in advance expecting success.

NOVEMBER

21

Opportunity will pass by an unprepared person. Prepare yourself for opportunities before they present themselves.

NOVEMBER

22

Take full responsibility, never complain and never explain.

NOVEMBER

23

Dress the way you wish to be addressed. How you present yourself is incredibly important. Present yourself in a respectable manner and you will be taken seriously. Dress like a prospect not a suspect.

NOVEMBER

24

If you want an extraordinary income, you must do extraordinary things.

NOVEMBER

25

In order to be successful, you must do today the things that others won't do, so that you can have the things tomorrow that others won't have.

NOVEMBER

26

Your life at present is not a true reflection of your real potential. There is more in you. You have greatness within you!

NOVEMBER

27

P ositivity is contagious!

NOVEMBER

28

Let your behaviour and mannerisms speak louder than your voice.

NOVEMBER

29

Study your own cultural history. It is a map that tells you where you have come from and potentially where you may be going.

NOVEMBER

30

Engage in continual personal development and surround yourself with people that help you grow, mentally, spiritually and financially.

DECEMBER

DECEMBER

1

Accept that most people don't know, that they don't know but they think that they know.

DECEMBER

2

Associate with strong accountability partners that tell you what you need to hear, not what you want to hear.

DECEMBER

3

What you think about is what you bring about.

DECEMBER

4

Develop an extraordinary interest in things, people and everything that you encounter.

DECEMBER

5

Success is not determined by your aptitude, success is determined by your attitude.

DECEMBER

6

Your tomorrow is determined by what you do today. What you are to be, you are now becoming.

DECEMBER

7

Ablunt pencil is better than a sharp mind. Always write your goals and ideas down on paper or keep a digital copy saved.

DECEMBER

8

Be curious about all things and develop an enthusiastic interest for life.

DECEMBER

9

The presence of God will give you boundless enthusiasm and vitality.

DECEMBER

10

The desire to live up to your higher self will help you identify what it takes to get on top of things and stay there.

DECEMBER

11

Avoid arguments and respond to negative attitudes with a positive, optimistic and loving countenance.

DECEMBER

12

Prepare for each day as though it was your last. Study, pray, think and visualise of your best life ever.

DECEMBER

13

The biggest war you will ever experience is the war between your two ears, The war that takes place in your mind.

DECEMBER

14

The most valuable asset you have is you. Take care of yourself first.

DECEMBER

15

A good positive, enthusiastic, attitude is a little thing that makes a big difference.

DECEMBER
16

Your own personal development is the biggest and best contribution you can make to your friends, family, field of work and the wider community.

DECEMBER

17

Congratulate yourself daily for your most recent accomplishments. This will encourage you to continue doing the little daily disciplines necessary to achieve your goals.

DECEMBER

18

Visualise your ideal lifestyle in detail. By doing this daily, you can take a regular trip to into your future. This will motivate you to remain disciplined in working your plan. Remind yourself of this vision whenever you hit a slump.

DECEMBER

19

What would be possible to you if you could have anything you wanted? Ponder, what you would do? Who would you become? How would you add value to your friends, family and wider community?

DECEMBER

20

Develop the necessary skills to make you an attractive person to the marketplace. It's not the skills you obtain that makes you valuable, it's the person you become by having those skills that makes you attractive.

DECEMBER

21

The more you become, the more you achieve and the more you achieve, the more you become.

DECEMBER

22

Love conquers all things. Greet today and everyday from this point onwards with love in your heart.

DECEMBER

23

If you do what is easy, your life will be hard. If you do what is hard, your life will be easy.

DECEMBER

24

Punctuality is key in your time management plan for success. If you arrive at least 10 minutes early, you are on time. If you arrive on time you are already late.

DECEMBER

25

Put God first, in everything that you do.

DECEMBER

26

Being realistic is mostly a negative frame of mind and the most common path to mediocrity.

DECEMBER

27

Allocate a regular time slot for refreshing your positive mindset. It's easy to become dull and worn by the normal insipid paradigm. Read, listen and watch material that promotes living an inspired lifestyle.

DECEMBER

28

F.E.A.R has two meanings. Forget Everything And Run. Face Everything And Rise. Use your F.E.A.R as fuel to push you forward.

DECEMBER

29

Just as you feed your body nutritious healthy food, feed your mind nourishing and wholesome thoughts.

DECEMBER

30

Y ou are greater than your challenges, within them lies hidden opportunities for you to gain more victories.

DECEMBER

31

When dealing with difficult people, remember that someones opinion of you does not have to become your reality. You are the architect of your own destiny and become what you think you are.

ABOUT THE AUTHOR

Dare Oduye is the author of the best seller *Abstract Expressionist Interior Spaces*. He received graduate and postgraduate training in Architecture and Architectural Engineering at the University of Westminster.

Dare is a product of the principles he reveals in Growth Mindset Daily and has provided lectures and seminars at a number of academic and professional institutions across the UK.

As a published Author, he has worked with industry experts, specialist organizations and manufacturers in the construction industry; to achieve regulatory compliance through sustainable building fabric solutions.

Dare's philosophy of positive thinking and personal development has influenced an unprecedented number of people from all walks of life, especially in the business and competitive sport environments.

Now, his philosophy and principles can be found within these pages. The messages are essential in the course of daily life, his book provides inspiration when you most need it and leads the way to a fuller, happier and more satisfying life.

More on Dare Oduye

To have Dare Oduye speak to your organization about the principles in Growth Mindset Daily or other personal development insights, email: dodezignsltd@gmail.com

www.dodezigns.com

This publication has been brought to you by Dodezigns. Dodezigns, seeks to provide quality educational inspiration and personal development to share with the world. We proudly strive to spread inspiration and promote positivity to others

Connect with the Dodezigns community of like-minded achievers online @dodezigns on the following platforms:

Made in United States
North Haven, CT
03 May 2023

36206885R00212